# Lila and Andy learn about

# Safety on Ice

Kenneth Adams

Book Cover by Kenneth Adams
Illustrations by Kenneth Adams
First Edition 2025

ISBN: 978-1-998552-11-5

Mistakes happen. Never stop trying.

Hi there! It's your favorite explorers, Andy and Lila again. Today we're spending time at our local lake. The lake is completely frozen over, just look at all the snow and ice. Isn't it beautiful? Winter is such an exciting time, full of fun adventures, like ice skating and sledding.

Living in Canada, we're pretty much winter experts! We've learned that, whether you're ice fishing, skating, or simply spending time near a frozen lake, it's very important to know how to stay safe on and around ice so you can enjoy winter activities without getting hurt.

Our dad is an Engineer who designs ice roads in the Arctic, and he's teaching us so much about ice safety. We can't wait to share what we know, so you always stay safe during your winter adventures.

Are you ready to learn? Let's get started!

# What is Ice?

You may have made ice cubes at home in the freezer, right? Well, ice is just frozen water. When it gets cold enough, water in ponds, lakes, rivers and streams turns from a liquid to a solid, which we call ice.

Unlike most other materials that get smaller when they freeze, water actually expands and becomes less dense when it turns to ice. That's why ice cubes float in your drink!

When a lake or pond starts to freeze, the ice forms from the top down, not from the bottom up. This is because the outside air temperature is much lower than the temperature of the water, so the top layer of the water freezes first.

Water reaches its maximum density at 39.2°F (4°C) and freezes at 32°F (0°C) to form ice. Since the ice is colder and less dense than liquid water, it floats on the surface. The floating ice then creates an insulating layer that helps prevent the water below from freezing. This allows deeper water to stay liquid during freezing conditions, which is important for fish and other creatures living in the water, since they can survive below the ice all winter long.

Did you know that the safest ice is found in areas with consistent temperatures below freezing for an extended period? Temperatures that change all the time, can make ice conditions very unstable.

Not all ice is the same though! Some ice is thick and strong and can support your weight. Other ice is thin and weak, and stepping on it could be dangerous. The strength of ice can change depending on how cold it is outside, how thick the ice is, what time of year it is, and whether water is moving under the ice. No matter what, where, or when, we always need to be very careful when we find ourselves on ice.

Have you ever seen cracks in ice? Cracks in ice are very common, and not all cracks are bad, but it could be a sign that the ice might not be safe. Even if it looks solid, it could break if you step on it. That's why it's so important to learn how to tell if ice is safe or not.

# The Dangers of Ice

Ice can be very slippery, so you can easily slip, fall, and hurt yourself. The most dangerous thing about ice is that it can break if it's not strong enough. Falling through ice is very scary! The freezing water can cause your body to lose heat very fast.

This is called hypothermia, and can make you very sick. Some of the symptoms of hypothermia to look out for are uncontrolled shivering, slow breathing, a slow heart rate, confusion and slurred speech.

Did you know that hypothermia can set in within minutes of falling into freezing water? The body loses heat 25 times faster in water than in air, making quick rescue critical.

Another danger is when there is fast-moving water under the ice. Water flowing in rivers and streams, and sometimes even in certain areas of lakes, can make the ice very weak or cause it to break. When you fall through the ice in an area where the water is moving, the current can pull you in under the ice, making it very difficult for you to find an opening in the ice to climb out from.

It is very important to remember that ice conditions can change quickly because of the weather. Ice that was safe yesterday, might not be safe today.

Did you know that temperature changes can dramatically affect ice thickness? A few days of mild weather can quickly weaken ice that previously seemed solid.

Ice near a bridge

Ice near the shoreline

Ice on a river

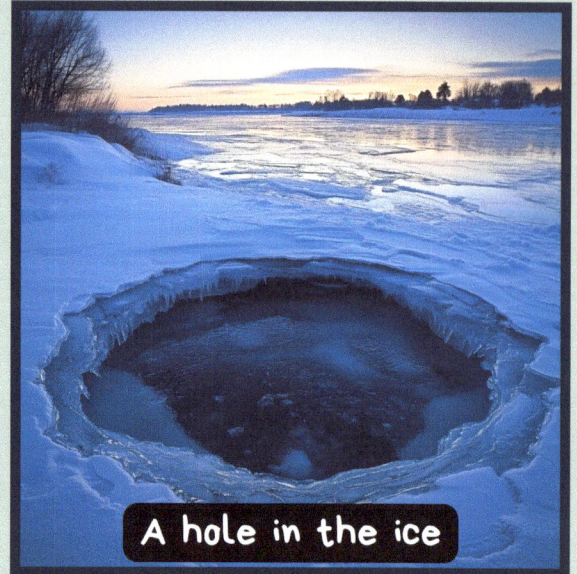
A hole in the ice

Certain areas on ice are more dangerous than others. We call these danger zones. Here are some danger zones you should avoid when traveling on ice.

**Near the shoreline:** Ice can be thinner along the shore due to heat from the land, and moving water.

**Bridge areas:** Since water may be moving under a bridge, the ice may form differently and could be thinner than elsewhere.

**Areas with overflow:** When water is flowing over the ice, it may be an indication that the ice is cracked or sinking.

**Dark, wet spots:** Dark areas on the ice may indicate thin ice or water on top.

**Cracks or holes:** Always stay away from these. When you make holes in the ice, like for ice fishing, always make sure everyone knows where they are, so nobody falls into them.

**Where rivers or creeks run under the ice:** The ice will be much weaker, especially where the water is flowing fast.

# Safe Practices on Ice

Never go onto the ice alone! Always go with, or ask permission from a responsible adult who understands the risks and safety procedures, just like how you ask your parents for permission before you go swimming or riding your bike around the neighborhood.

If no adults are going with you, take a couple of friends, and make sure Mom and Dad know where you are. Use the buddy system, where everyone is responsible for looking out for everyone else in the group.

Before stepping onto the ice, you should always know the thickness of the ice, because ice needs a certain thickness to support your weight.

During the winter, many municipalities with waterbodies like lakes and ponds in their jurisdiction, test ice thickness and share the information with the public. Check with local authorities or park services for any warnings, rules, or the current condition of the ice.

If you can't find information about the ice thickness, always make sure to test the thickness of the ice by using an ice auger or chisel. If you are traveling over a lake, or when you move away from an area already tested, remember to test again. To stay safe, you should check the ice thickness as often as possible.

If a river or creek is under the ice, the ice will be much weaker, especially where the water is flowing quickly. A good place to cross will have thick, hard ice that looks clear or blue. Stay away from danger zones, like areas with cracks, or areas where the ice looks milky, flaky, or bubbly.

When walking on ice, take short steps to stay balanced, walk slowly and carefully, and pay attention to the ice in front of you.

Avoid going out on the ice at night or when it's foggy. It is very dangerous to be on ice that you can't see.

If you hear cracking sounds, or if you see water flowing over or under the ice, or if there are other warning signs, get off the ice as quickly as you can safely do so!

# Testing Ice Safely

Now comes the really important part of how to know if ice is safe. Dad taught us the "THINK, TEST, then STEP" rule.

<u>THINK</u>: Before stepping on the ice, ask yourself these questions:

- What's the weather been like lately?

- What time of day is it?

- Has the ice been frozen for a long time?

- Am I close to potential danger zones?

- Do I see any warning signs, like cracks, slush or open water?

- Are other people using the ice safely?

- Do I have the right safety gear?

- Am I alone or with others?

- Do I know how to get off the ice if something goes wrong?

By asking yourself these questions, you are assessing whether it is worth the risk to go onto the ice. This is called a risk assessment, and by answering the questions honestly, you can make good decisions to avoid bad situations or accidents on the ice.

The following ice thickness requirements are given as a general guideline only. Always be sure to check with local authorities on ice thickness requirements before going onto the ice.

For walking:
4 inches or 10 centimeters

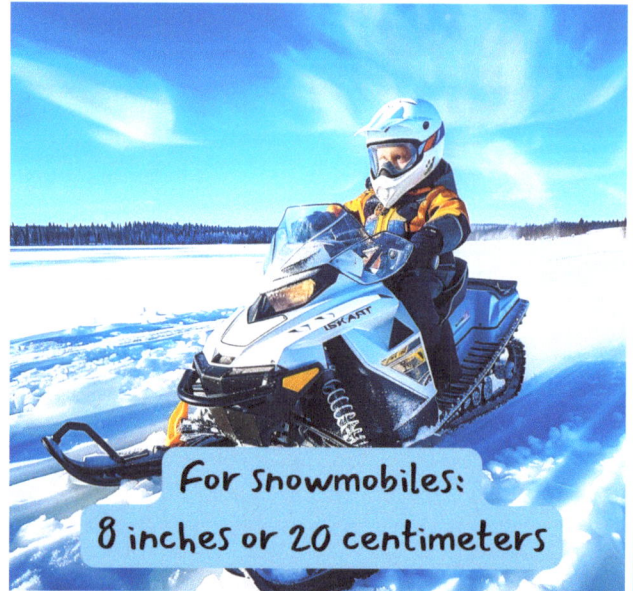
For snowmobiles:
8 inches or 20 centimeters

For small cars:
12 inches or 30 centimeters

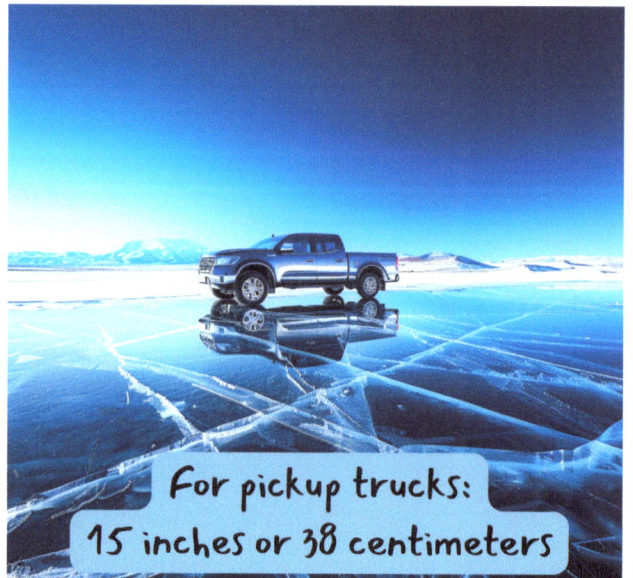
For pickup trucks:
15 inches or 38 centimeters

**TEST:** Check the color and thickness of the ice.

- Color
  - Naturally formed clear blue ice is usually the strongest.
  - Overflow ice or white, cloudy, snow ice can be weaker and unreliable.

- Knowing the ice thickness is very important if you want to stay safe on ice.

- Ice thickness rules may change depending on where you are. Always be sure to check with local authorities on ice thickness requirements before going onto the ice.

- Testing ice thickness should never be done alone, and never by kids. Always have an experienced grown-up around before going onto any frozen water that has not been tested. Adults know how to check if the ice is safe and they have the right tools to do it. Your job is to watch, listen, and learn from them. Remember, ice can be tricky, and even ice that looks safe can be dangerous.

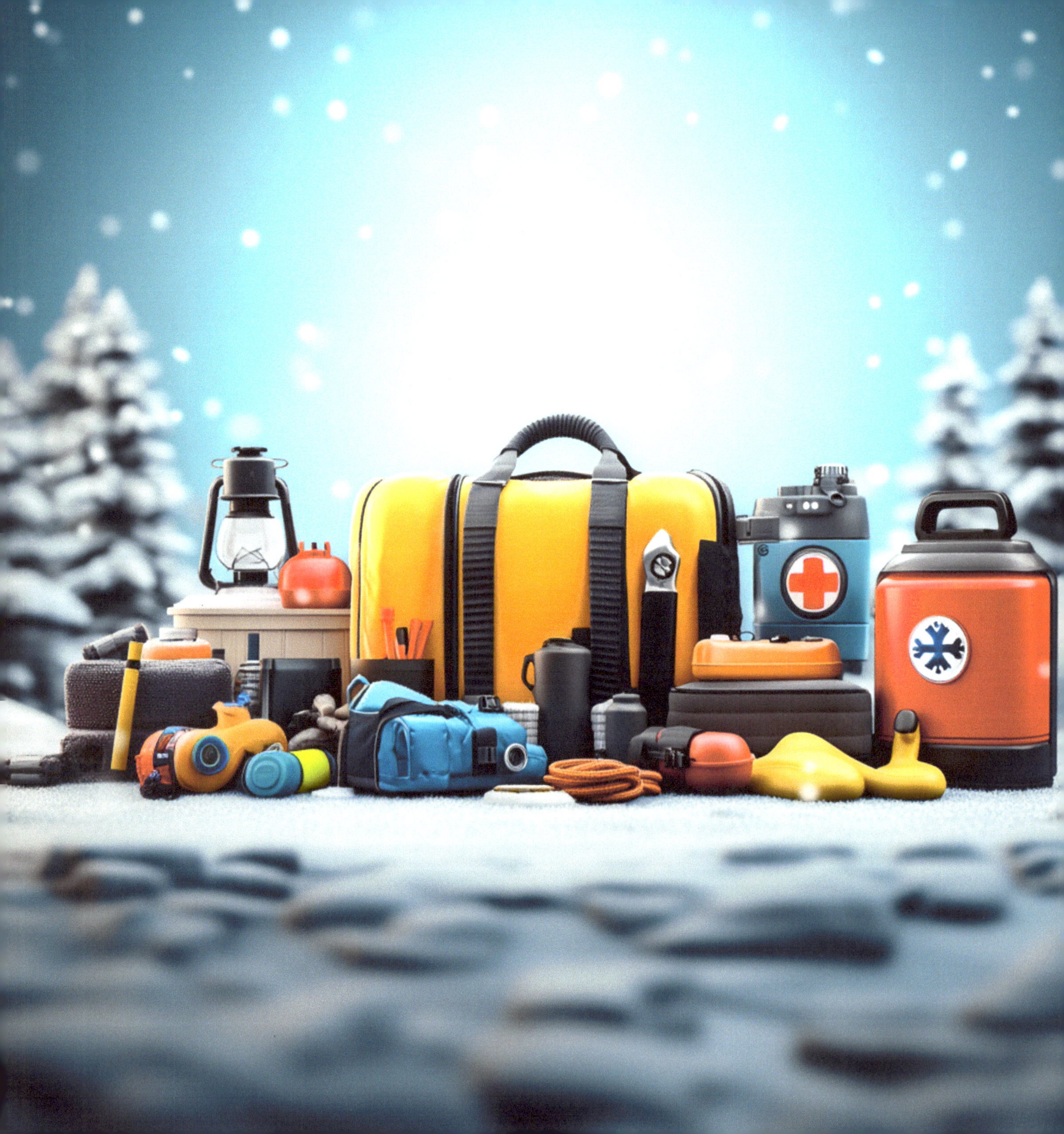

STEP: Once it is confirmed the ice is safe:
- Proceed with caution. Walk slowly, distributing your weight evenly over the ice.
- Carry a safety kit, including ice picks, a throw rope, and a flotation device, to prepare for emergencies.
- Avoid traveling alone. Having a companion increases safety in case of accidents.

An ice chisel

An ice auger

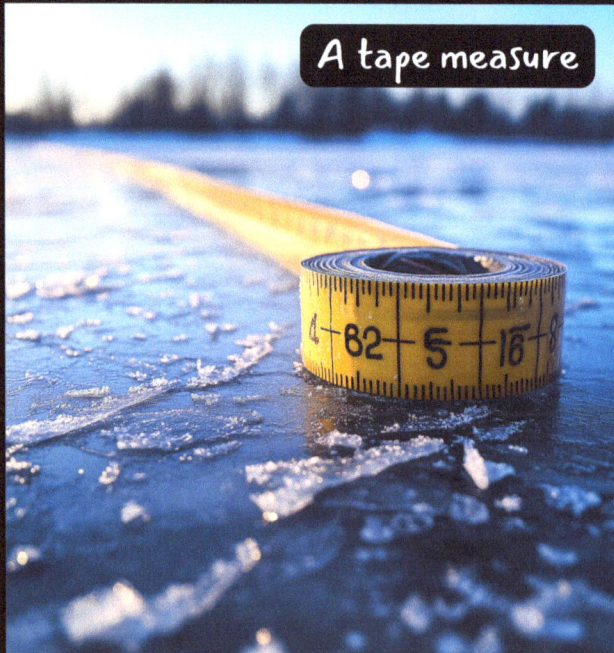

A tape measure

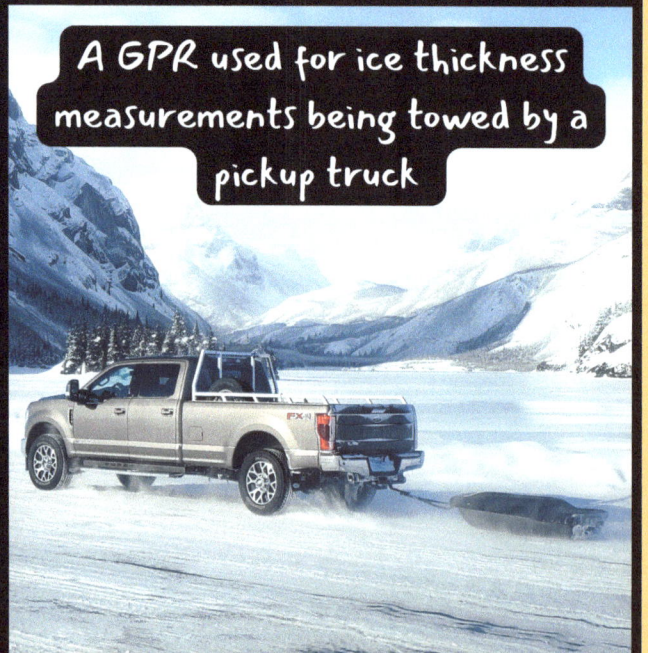

A GPR used for ice thickness measurements being towed by a pickup truck

Some of the ice testing equipment used by adults to determine ice thickness and ice safety includes:

**Ice Chisel:** This is like a strong stick with a metal point. You can use it to carefully chip at the ice to check its color and gauge its strength and thickness based on how easily it breaks.

**Ice Auger:** This is a hand-operated drill that bore holes in the ice. Ice augers can be very dangerous, and should not be used without permission. It is safest to allow Mom or Dad to use the auger instead.

**Tape Measure or Stick:** After drilling a hole, you can use this to check the ice thickness. Be careful not to drop the measuring tape or stick down the hole!

**Ground Penetrating Radar:** The use of ground penetrating radar is a highly advanced method that uses electromagnetic waves to scan the ice. GPR can provide very accurate and detailed data on ice thickness and ice conditions without having to drill holes. It's very useful, especially when you have to measure the ice thickness over large areas, like public skating rinks.

# Ice Safety Gear

When going out on the ice, it is very important to dress properly. Wearing layers of clothing helps to keep you warm.

- Use warm hats, toques, or beanies that cover your ears.
- Make sure you have waterproof gloves or mittens to keep your hands dry. Always remember to bring an extra pair, just in case.
- The socks you choose are extremely important. Synthetic materials like polyester or nylon blends, wick away moisture and keep your feet comfortable. Merino wool socks are soft and insulating, and can keep your feet nice and toasty. Try to avoid cotton socks, as they retain moisture, which can make your feet very cold.
- Use insulated boots with a good grip to prevent slipping on the ice.
- Try to wear brightly colored clothing. This way you will be easily seen against the white backdrop of the snow and ice.
- A safety helmet is a good idea to protect your head in case of a fall, whether you're skating, sledding, or snowmobiling. In some cases, wearing a helmet is mandatory when you are out enjoying winter activities on ice. Always make sure to know what the requirements are before you head out.

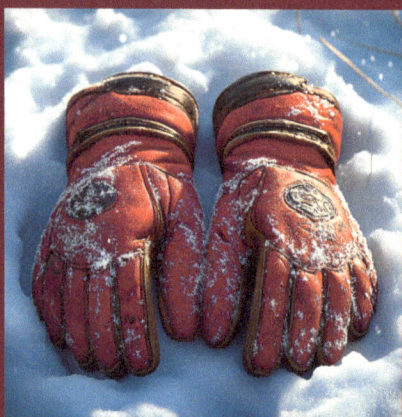

Other safety equipment and smart technology that can be useful when you plan to spend a day on the ice include:

- Ice picks or claws, for pulling yourself out of the water if you fall through the ice.
- Rope that can be used to pull someone out of the water, safely from the shoreline.
- Life jackets or PFDs (Personal Flotation Devices) that can keep you afloat in the water.
- A cell phone or a whistle to call for help in an emergency. Remember to keep your cell phone in a waterproof bag or case, and make sure the battery is fully charged.
- A portable battery pack or power bank as backup power for your phone during cold weather. Batteries drain much faster in cold temperatures.
- A GPS device or smartphone app that can mark safe routes and track your location, even in areas with poor cell service.
- Local weather apps that send alerts about changing conditions and ice safety warnings.
- Ice thickness measurement apps that help you log and share ice conditions with other winter adventurers in your area.
- A compass or navigation app as backup, since GPS signals can sometimes be unreliable in remote areas.
- Emergency notification apps that can quickly share your location with emergency services if you need help.

Remember that while technology is helpful, it should never replace basic safety practices or proper adult supervision.

Always make sure your devices are fully charged before heading out, and don't rely solely on electronic devices for safety. They can be very unreliable due to extreme cold or poor network availability.

# In Case of Emergency

Accidents can happen, even when you're careful. Here's what to do if you fall through the ice.

- Don't panic. Try to stay calm, kick with your legs, and keep your head above water.
- Shout for help. Yell loudly, or use your whistle so someone can hear you and come to help you.
- Don't try to remove your winter clothing. While heavy clothes can hinder your ability to move around, they can also trap air to provide warmth and flotation.
- Turn towards the direction you came from.
- Place your hands and arms on the unbroken ice surface. Use your elbows or ice pick to grip the edge of the ice. Kick your legs to push your body onto the ice. If your clothes have trapped a lot of water, you may have to lift yourself partially out of the water on your elbows to let the water drain before crawling forward.
- Roll, don't walk. Once you're out, lie flat on the ice and roll away from the hole. This spreads your weight and reduces the risk of breaking the ice again.
- Get warm as soon as possible. Head indoors right away, remove wet clothes and warm up with blankets or dry clothes.

Rescue workers conducting Ice Rescue Training

Here's what to do when you see someone else fall through the ice.

- Stay calm. In a calm, clear voice, tell the person in the water not to panic, and to slowly breathe in through the nose and out through the mouth.
- Call for help immediately. Unless you are alone, or had special ice rescue training, you should never attempt to rescue someone by yourself.
- Do not run onto the ice or walk towards the broken ice. Instead, lie down on the ice to distribute your weight and avoid breaking through yourself.
- Reach out to the person who has fallen through the ice with anything they can grab onto, like a fishing rod, a long stick, a rope, or a jacket.
- Tell them to kick their feet, and keep their head above the water.
- Pull the person out carefully using the fishing rod, stick, rope, or jacket.
- Once the person is out of the water, wrap them in warm blankets to stop their body from losing heat, change them into dry clothes, and get them to a warm place as soon as you can.

Emergency
Contacts

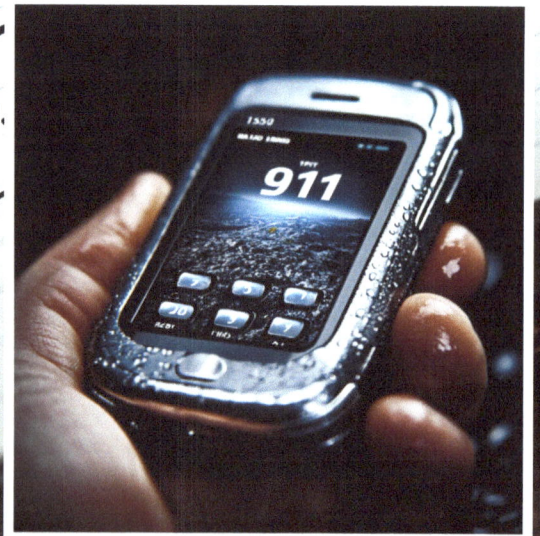

Before going out on the ice, it's important to be prepared for emergencies. Having the right contact information ready can help you get help quickly if something goes wrong.

Here's what you and your family should do:

- Make sure at least one of you keeps a list of emergency numbers on a phone. Also write it down on a waterproof card, just in case your phones get wet or stop working in the cold.

- Important numbers include:
  - Your local emergency services number. In most areas of Canada and the United States, this is 911.
  - The local police or fire department non-emergency number.
  - The nearest ranger station or park office number.
  - Your parents' or guardians' phone numbers.
  - Contact information for trusted neighbors or nearby family friends.

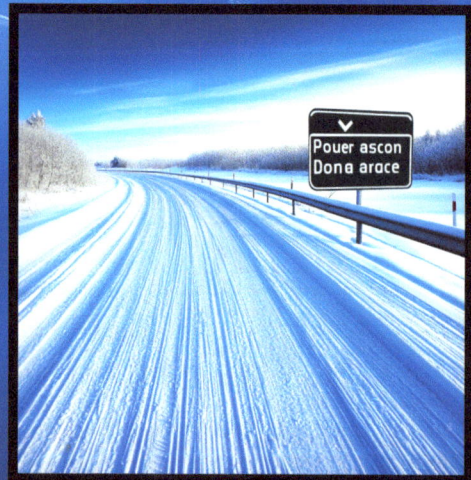

Tell someone who's not going with you, where you're going before heading out on the ice. Try to give them as much information as possible, like:

- Which lake, pond, or area you'll be going to.
- Where on the ice you plan to be, like "the west side near the campgrounds".
- What time you're leaving and when you plan to be back.
- Who else is going with you.
- What activities you're planning like skating, ice fishing, etc.

Know how to describe where you are in case you need help:

- Learn the names of nearby landmarks like bridges, buildings, or big trees.
- Be on the lookout for warning or information signs around the area.
- Look for mileage markers or trail names.
- Download maps on your phone that work without internet connection.
- Take note of any nearby street names or intersections.

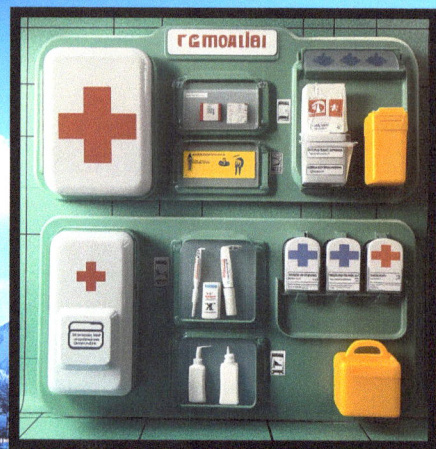

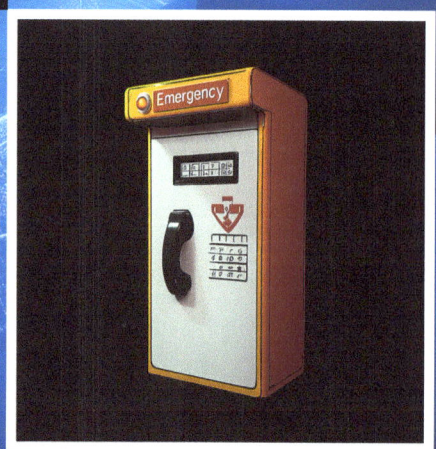

If you're in a popular ice fishing or skating area, find out if there are:

- Emergency phones or help stations nearby.
- First aid stations or warming huts.
- Local patrol services that monitor the ice.
- Posted emergency information boards with contact numbers.

Remember, in an emergency, every minute counts! Having this information available can help others to find you quickly if you need help. Make sure everyone in your group knows where to find the emergency contact information and how to use it.

Ice can be so much fun when you know how to stay safe! Winter activities on ice include things like skating and ice fishing, and it is very important to always make sure you have the correct equipment.

Remember, the best adventures are the ones where everyone stays safe. Always respect the ice, be aware of the risks, and make sure to follow all the rules we discussed today.

Share what you have learned with your family and friends so they can stay safe too. By learning about ice safety, you're already on your way to being a winter safety expert.

Bye, everyone! Stay safe, stay warm, and enjoy your adventures!

# Ice Safety Quiz

## Multiple Choice Questions

1. What happens to water when it freezes into ice?
   a) It becomes more dense
   b) It becomes less dense and expands
   c) It maintains the same density
   d) It shrinks in size

2. At what temperature does water freeze?
   a) 39.2°F (4°C)
   b) 32°F (0°C)
   c) 28°F (−2°C)
   d) 35°F (1.7°C)

3. When a lake starts to freeze, where does ice form first?
   a) From the bottom up
   b) From the middle out
   c) From the top down
   d) All at once throughout

4. What is the minimum ice thickness recommended for walking?
   a) 2 inches
   b) 4 inches
   c) 6 inches
   d) 8 inches

5. Which type of ice is usually the strongest?
   a) White, cloudy ice
   b) Clear blue ice
   c) Snow ice
   d) Overflow ice

6. It's safe to go on ice alone as long as you have proper safety gear.
   True or False?

7. Ice conditions that were safe yesterday will always be safe today.
   True or False?

8. Cotton socks are the best choice for ice activities because they keep feet warm.
   True or False?

9. You should remove your winter clothing immediately if you fall through ice.
   True or False?

10. Dark spots on ice may indicate thin ice or water on top.
    True or False?

## Fill in the Blank Questions

11. The minimum ice thickness required for small cars is _____ inches.

12. When getting out of the water after falling through ice, you should _____ away from the hole rather than walk.

13. Water reaches its maximum density at _____ °F (4°C).

14. _____ is a condition where your body loses heat very fast in cold water.

15. The "Think, _____, then Step" rule is important for ice safety.

## Short Answer Questions

16. List three items that should be in an ice safety kit.

17. What are two characteristics of unsafe ice that you should look out for?

18. Name three "danger zones" where ice is likely to be thinner or weaker.

19. What should you do first if you see someone fall through the ice?

20. Explain the proper way to check ice thickness. Who should perform this check?

## Emergency Response Questions

21. What is the first thing you should do if you fall through the ice?

22. When helping someone who has fallen through ice, why should you lie down on the ice?

23. After getting out of cold water, what are the immediate steps you should take?

24. What information should you share with someone before going out on the ice?

25. Why should you avoid traveling alone on ice?

## Safety Equipment Questions

26. Name three types of clothing layers recommended for ice activities.

27. Why is it important to wear brightly colored clothing on ice?

28. What type of communication devices should you carry when on ice?

29. Why should you keep your cell phone in a waterproof bag?

30. What are two types of tools used to test ice thickness?

# Answers

1. b)
2. b)
3. c)
4. b)
5. b)

6. False
7. False
8. False
9. False
10. True

11. 12 inches
12. Roll
13. 39.2
14. Hypothermia
15. Test

16. Ice picks/claws, rope, and life jacket/PFD
17. Cracks in the ice, dark spots, moving water underneath
18. Near shoreline, bridge areas, areas where rivers/creeks flow under ice
19. Stay calm and call for help
20. Use an ice auger or chisel; only adults should perform the check
21. Don't panic and try to stay calm
22. To distribute weight and avoid breaking through
23. Get indoors, remove wet clothes, warm up with blankets or dry clothes
24. Location, planned activities, expected return time, who you're with
25. To have help available in case of emergency
26. Base layer, insulating layer, outer waterproof layer
27. To be easily visible against snow and ice
28. Cell phone and whistle
29. To protect it from water damage in case of emergency
30. Ice chisel and ice auger

Take a look at the other subjects Lila and Andy are learning about...

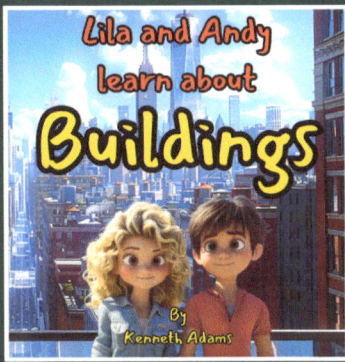
Lila and Andy learn about **Buildings**
By Kenneth Adams

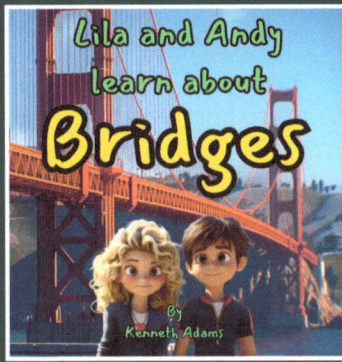
Lila and Andy learn about **Bridges**
By Kenneth Adams

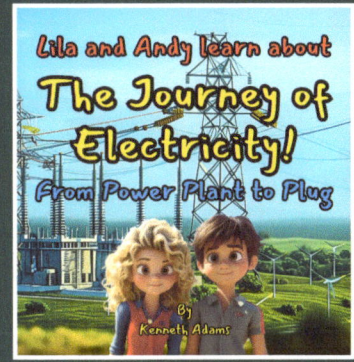
Lila and Andy learn about **The Journey of Electricity!**
From Power Plant to Plug
By Kenneth Adams

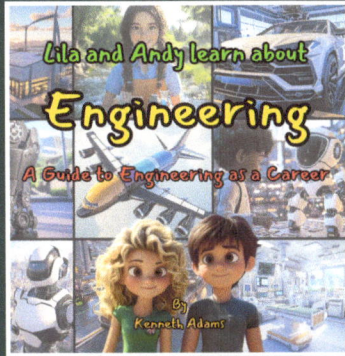
Lila and Andy learn about **Engineering**
A Guide to Engineering as a Career
By Kenneth Adams

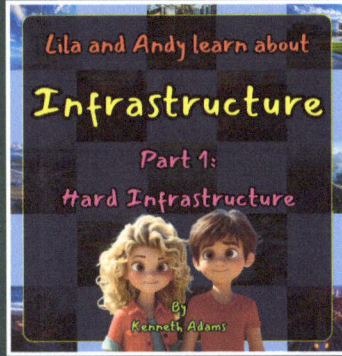
Lila and Andy learn about **Infrastructure**
Part 1: Hard Infrastructure
By Kenneth Adams

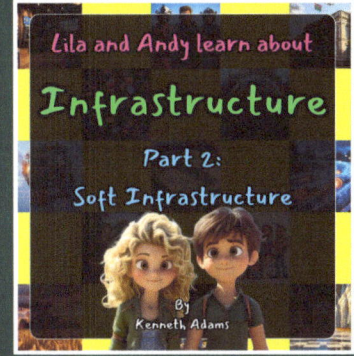
Lila and Andy learn about **Infrastructure**
Part 2: Soft Infrastructure
By Kenneth Adams

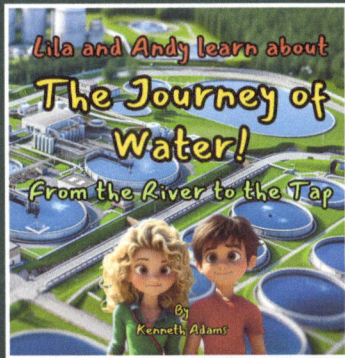
Lila and Andy learn about **The Journey of Water!**
From the River to the Tap
By Kenneth Adams

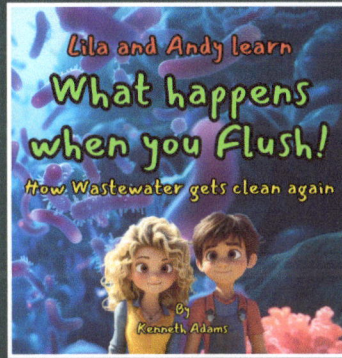
Lila and Andy learn **What happens when you Flush!**
How Wastewater gets clean again
By Kenneth Adams

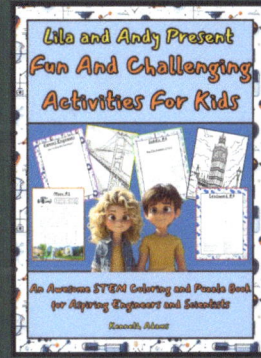
Lila and Andy Present **Fun And Challenging Activities For Kids**
An Awesome STEM Coloring and Puzzle Book for Aspiring Engineers and Scientists
Kenneth Adams

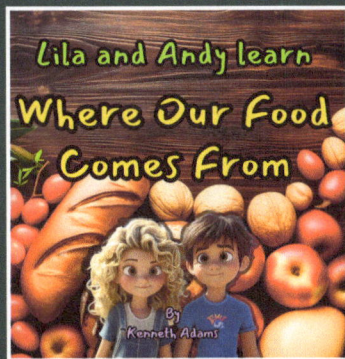
Lila and Andy learn **Where Our Food Comes From**

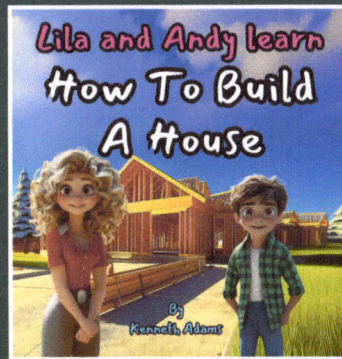
Lila and Andy learn **How To Build A House**
By Kenneth Adams

Lila and Andy learn about **Recycling**

www.ingramcontent.com/pod-product-compliance
Lightning Source LLC
LaVergne TN
LVHW072134070426

835513LV00003B/97

*9781998552115*